The Future ABC Song

CITI OF
BOOKS

CITIOFBOOKS, INC.
3736 Eubank NE Suite A1
Albuquerque, NM 87111-3579
wwwww.citiofbooks.com
Hotline: 1 (877) 389-2759
Fax: 1 (505) 930-7244

Ordering Information:
Quantity sales. Special discounts are available on quantity purchases by corporations, associations, and others. For details, contact the publisher at the address above.

Printed in the United States of America.
ISBN-13:   Paperback   979-8-89391-671-3
               eBook   979-8-89391-672-0

Library of Congress Control Number: 2025908875

LATER THAT DAY...
I,...
CAN'T REMEMBER...
IS IT A,D ,F, J, UM OR IS
IT A,C, D.

IT'S 3:00 .
IT'S TIME TO GO
HOME NOW.

Parents please scan the QR code with your phone to hear the song with your child

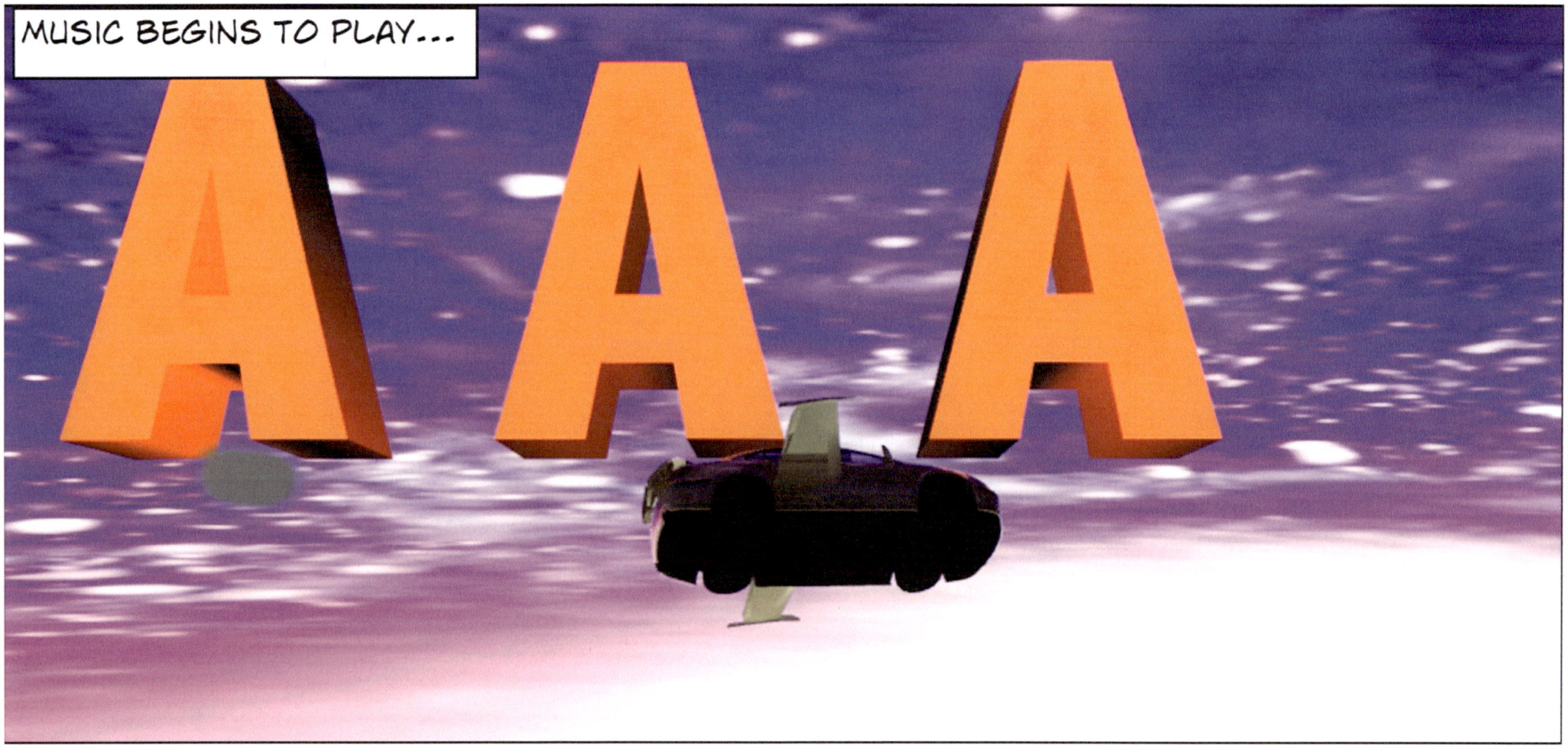

MUSIC BEGINS TO PLAY...

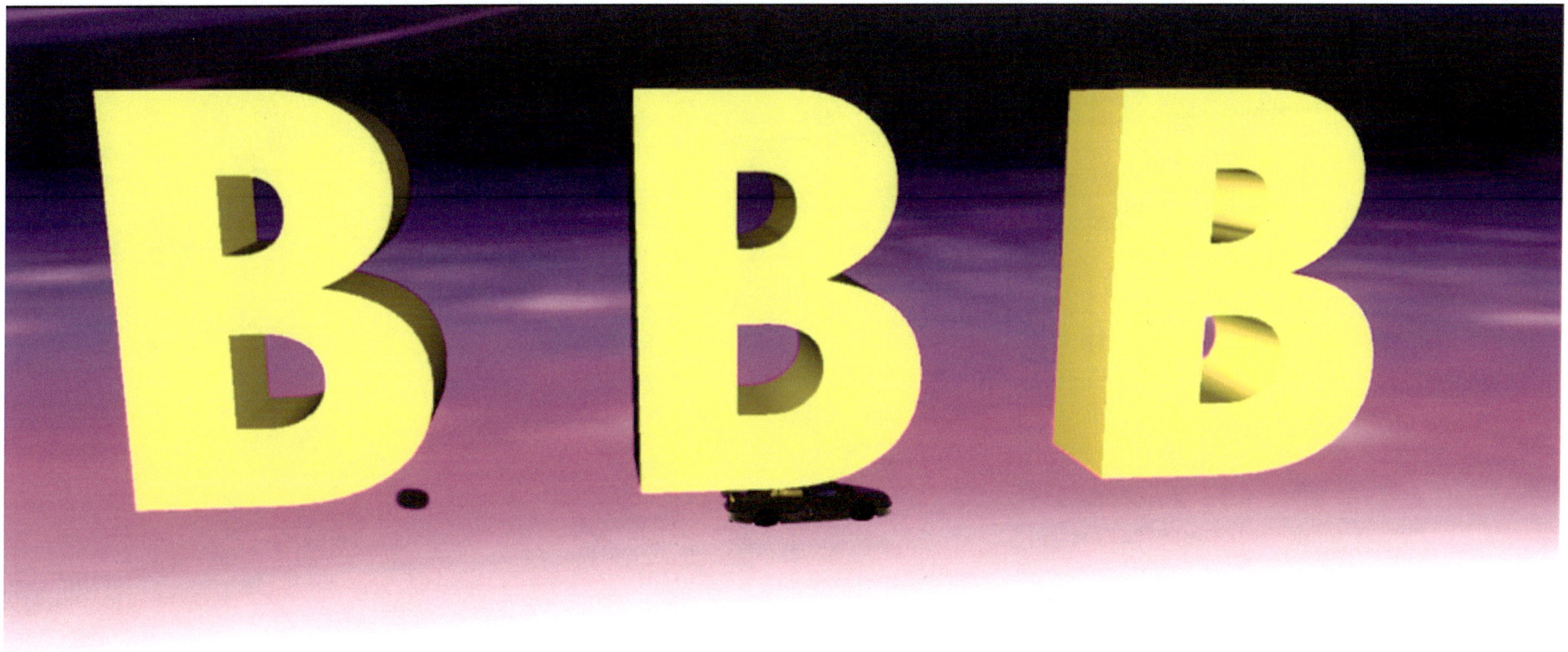
B B B

THE SONG PLAYS AGAIN

ABOUT THE AUTHORS

MARUMBA JONES - DAVIS
AUTHOR

Marumba Jones - Davis is a mother of 3 an assistant educator and a wig enhancement designer. This is her first published book. She and Mr. Blackshear Jr. were co-workers and have previously worked on and educational children's ABC video which can be seen on YouTube.

https://.youtu.be/MaAeUlrAqSM

HENRY BLACKSHEAR JR.
ILLUSTRATOR

Henry Blackshear Jr. is an Artist, Illustrator, Writer, Puppeteer and Craft Creator. This is his forth collaborative published book. He has worked as a professional illustrator for 10 years and presently freelances as an illustrator and an animator.